CINEPHILIA

Assorted film criticism, 2009-2010

by Benjamin Kerstein

Contents

The Incredible Awesomeness of Michael Bay

Everyone who writes about movies is now apparently required to hate Michael Bay. The ex-director of commercials and music videos, who has made some of the most successful films of the last decade—*Bad Boys*, *The Rock*, *Armageddon*, *Transformers*, etc.—has become, without a doubt, the *bête noir* of modern cinema; or at least of modern movie critics. The critical establishment has never really liked Michael Bay, but the recent release of *Transformers: Revenge of the Fallen*, which despite having been demolished by every respectable critic on both sides of the Atlantic, is hurtling swiftly toward the box-office stratosphere, was unquestionably the nail in the coffin.

The best invective from this critical night of the long knives probably belongs to the *Guardian's* Peter Bradshaw, who described the film as "like watching paint dry while getting hit over the head with a frying pan." He was hardly alone, however. The always reliable Roger Ebert went so far as to echo Bradshaw's kitchenware allegory when he called the film "a horrible experience of unbearable length, briefly punctuated by three or four amusing moments…. If you want to save yourself the ticket price, go into the kitchen, cue up a male choir singing the music of hell, and get a kid to start banging pots and pans together. Then close your eyes and use your imagination." Manhola Dargis of the *New York Times* chose brevity over references to household implements, and described the film with the single word "cretinous."

The ire directed toward the film, however, has mostly taken second place to an unabashed hysterical loathing of its director. For example, Salon.com's Stephanie Zacharek's review began:

> "He's here—I smell him." That's a line from Transformers:
> Revenge of the Fallen, but funnily enough, it's also what I
> think every time I sit down to watch a Michael Bay movie….
> Bay is a purveyor of clunky, occasionally enjoyable crap: I

sometimes get pleasure out of his movies by marveling at the astonishingly low level of craftsmanship that he consistently gets away with.... And maybe Revenge of the Fallen is no worse than any other Bay movie: You probably can't sink much lower after making a piece of pseudo-historical hokum like Pearl Harbor. Still, big, dumb and clumsy is no way to go through life.

Referring to Bay's treatment of star Megan Fox, Zarachek continued "She makes her entrance crouched on the seat of a motorcycle, her pert butt aimed at the heavens. Later in the movie, a once-aggressive robot she's befriended and tamed eagerly humps her leg. This is what it means, in the Bay universe, to be a movie sex symbol."

Incompetence, barbarism, and misogyny, however, were least among the various complaints. Robert Wilonsky of the *Village Voice* accused the director of jingoistic self-plagiarism and outright cinematic sadism.

You may recall that its 2007 predecessor was a mostly capable commercial for Transformers toys and Bay's previous films, from which most of the iconography was lifted as the man continues to pay homage to his favorite filmmaker. (Has he ever made a movie without the image of fluttering American flags?).... But why speak when you can SCREAM [sic] for almost two and a half hours? Why go subtle when there's shit to blow up...? But a respite's not to be—not when the Fallen's gotten back up after a 19,000-year rest somewhere in orbit around the earth, which he's looking to destroy, just because he can. Kind of like Michael Bay.

Wilonsky's final hint that Bay is not only a bad filmmaker, but a threat to civilization itself was made explicit by Chris Tookey in the *Daily Mail*, who remarked that "Bay is at his most obnoxious when he shows gigantic machines casually destroying icons of Ancient Egyptian civilization. Some may find this a depressingly accurate metaphor for what people like him are doing to our own culture."

4

It must be admitted that almost everything the critics have said about *Revenge of the Fallen* is true to a certain extent. Bay is most certainly unsubtle, lowbrow, and unapologetically mercenary. Ironically, however, the critics' belief that Bay is also a threat to all things decent and civilized in the world, the unabashed critical contempt and hatred that has been directed his way from the beginning of his career, says very little about Bay himself. Instead, it says almost everything about the pathetic state of American film criticism.

It was probably dissident film critic Armond White who sounded the first alarm in 2000, when he went to the barricades for controversial director Brian De Palma and his much-maligned *Mission to Mars*.

> Brian De Palma's critical drubbing over *Mission to Mars*—reminiscent of the scene in *Airplane!* where passengers line up to smack an old lady—is the clearest evidence of the catastrophe that has befallen contemporary film criticism. *Mission to Mars* is a litmus test. It can be said with certainty that any reviewer who pans it does not understand movies, let alone like them. They'd be better off reviewing static, juvenile media like television or comic books.

White, while unquestionably correct, was somewhat premature. As has now been proven beyond a shadow of a doubt, the real litmus test is Michael Bay.

Michael Bay's films are not great. Most of them are not even particularly good in any serious way, but with the exception of *Pearl Harbor*—the director's one misbegotten bid for mainstream respectability—it is impossible to actively dislike any of them. The reason for this, I think, is that while Bay is certainly a hack in terms of story, character, and even plausibility, he is most certainly not a hack in the one area that really matters in cinema: visual spectacle.

Put simply, Michael Bay's films look extraordinary. One can go even further than that, and say that at certain points his images achieve moments of beauty that can only be described as transcendent. The fact that these images are couched in the idiom of the modern blockbuster action film, with all of their shortcomings, should not, as it does for so many, distract us from an appreciation of the fact that Bay may well be a hack in many areas, but he is not a hack—or even a gifted journeyman—in the realm of visual spectacle. He is, in fact, an artist, and an extraordinarily gifted one.

This can be difficult for the average critic to grasp, because like most commercial filmmakers, Bay's art is one of pieces and not the whole. His gift appears in fragmentary moments for which the film—that is, the story, the characters, etc.—are merely a vehicle, not the thing in itself. In Bay's case, these moments are almost all images; whether the opening sequence of *The Rock*, with its rain-drenched images of a military funeral played over Ed Harris' narration, or *Armageddon*'s penultimate montage of sun-drenched images of all those threatened by the end of the world. Moreover, some of these images are achieved through pure light and shade, with none of the slow-motion or computer-generated pyrotechnics with which Bay's name is constantly associated: the image of a newly redeemed Djimon Honsou emerging from underground into the brightness of a liberation he has helped engineer in *The Island*, or the extraordinary close-up of Admiral Yamamoto's sunken visage, defeated in his moment of triumph, as he intones the apocryphal line about awakening a sleeping giant in *Pearl Harbor*. Nonetheless, Bay's talent for the visceral power of images is sometimes contained in those very pyrotechnics the critics so despise. As adolescent as such pleasures may be, it cannot be denied that the scene in *Transformers* of Optimus Prime smashing through a truck, deploying a laser sword, and slashing his enemy's throat is a dazzling piece of kinetic filmmaking. A hack, by definition, is incapable of such things.

Also rarely remarked upon is the fact that amidst the carnage and stupidity the critics decry, Bay's films often contain some above-average acting. Ed Harris and Sean Connery in *The Rock* both deliver brilliant and at times surprisingly understated star turns; Sean Bean and Djimon Hounsou in *The Island* are both spellbinding, particularly Honsou, who gets a spine-tingling moment in which he tells Bean how he was marked as a child so that others would know he was less than human; Jon Voight frankly becomes FDR in *Pearl Harbor*, perfectly capturing the paralyzed statesman's unique combination of pathos and gravitas; and a case be made for John Turturro's comic turns in the *Transformers* films as masterpieces of modern camp.

Even the most-maligned of Bay's sins, his treatment of women, is in fact one of his greatest strengths. Since the silent era, the transformation of women in glittering, iconic erotic objects has been essential to the language of cinema. Eschewing the ice-queen tradition perfected by Hitchcock, Bay shoots his women for an immediate, absolute carnal beauty, the raw maximization of the female embraced by directors like Howard Hawks. Megan Fox's native charms are undeniable, but without Bay's camera, which both distances the viewer and hones in on her feral sexuality like a microscope, she would not be the less-than-obscure object of desire she is today.

In short, whatever Michael Bay's sins may be, the sum of his talents definitely adds up to a kind of cinema. This cinema is what Sergio Leone referred to as "cinema cinema," that is, cinema for its own sake, cinema in and for itself, cinema that exists for no other reason than to be cinema. Cinema as cinema is best expressed by the famous quote from Jean-Luc Godard's *Pierrot le Fou*: "A film is like a battleground. It has love, hate, action, violence and death. In one word: emotion."

Michael Bay's entire cinematic language consists of nothing but love, hate, action, violence, and death, and every one of his films is self-evidently a battleground. They are pure visual pageantry, possessed of an élan that seems to be nothing less than a cry of love for cinema as cinema. And this is precisely why the critics hate him.

White was certainly on to something when he said that most film critics do not "understand movies, let alone like them," but he did not go far enough. The truth is that most film critics hate movies. The type of cinema that most critics love is, essentially, a kind of anti-cinema. It is a cinema that hates itself, that cannot abide being cinema, and wants desperately to be something else. It shares something, then, with its champions, most of whom would prefer to be something other than movie critics, and who see film as — at best — a lowbrow substitute for more substantial art forms, such as literature, painting, dance, etc. In their eyes, cinema is clumsy, immature, populist, and corrupted by earthly success. This is how execrable illustrated novels like *The English Patient* or profoundly asinine works of pseudo social commentary like *American Beauty* managed to garner critical raves and Oscar nominations while genuine cinematic poetry like *Once Upon a Time in the West* and *2001* were savaged upon release. It is no coincidence that the current critical worship of Stanley Kubrick — the greatest of all the masters of cinema cinema — is overwhelmingly revisionist in nature; when his films first came out, the critics hated almost every single one of them.

This collective degradation and derangement of the critical establishment—of which Bay is hardly the only victim—may ultimately turn out to be a positive development. It is not impossible that something like the 1950s nouvelle vague, in which a younger generation of French film critics like Francois Truffaut and the aforementioned Godard stepped forward to defend cinema as cinema, may occur in the Anglophone world. They may not love Michael Bay, but they will hopefully recognize his esoteric virtues, just as their predecessors sang the praises of Howard Hawks, John Ford, and Alfred Hitchcock, once also derided as mere journeymen technicians. Until then, we must be content with the schadenfreude that comes from watching the continuing meltdown of a decadent establishment, as they heap their praises on the next excruciatingly dull adaptation of a Jane Austen novel or the latest utterly artless documentary by Michael Moore. The rest of us will be too busy attending Michael Bay or Zack Snyder's newest blockbuster, happily sharpening our oyster knives.

Originally published on August 1, 2009

Star Trek For the Masses

Review of *Star Trek*, directed by J.J. Abrams

No one who did not grow up with a Trekkie can possibly understand the hold the series has on its true believers. While my father is, at best, a middling fan (he never, for instance, took the time to learn the Klingon language), I was nevertheless compelled to spend a great deal of my childhood in the presence of *Star Trek* and its seemingly endless parade of spinoffs, each more second-rate than the last. There was *Star Trek: The Next Generation*, then *Deep Space Nine*, then something else, and I'm fairly certain there was something else after that, and Wikipedia claims there was also an animated series (before my time) and, of course, the feature films (eleven at last count).

Despite, or perhaps because, of my long and reluctant relationship with the franchise, I must admit that the willingness of fans to sit through these endless hours of *Trek* upon *Trek* upon *Trek* still mystifies me. There seems to be an almost limitless appetite, on the part of some people, for such things as large, talking, malevolent clouds of gas, unbearably sanctimonious political bromides, often wretched special effects, endless variations on the complications of time travel, and actors in rubber suits pretending to be suspiciously humanoid aliens. The willingness of the rest of us to do so, however, seems to have been understandably declining over time, which is probably why J.J. Abrams was hired to perform the now ubiquitous Hollywood "reboot" that every moribund franchise must undergo in order to reenter the cultural mainstream.

Abrams's efforts have been met, as everyone now knows, with immense success, mainly because he has dispensed with almost everything that made the series unbearable to semi-normal human beings—the endless complications of time travel remain, taken to their logical extreme. *Star Trek* in Abrams's and his writers' hands is the biggest Buck Rogers movie ever made; a rollicking thrill-ride through the space opera genre, with more starships exploding and lasers blasting per second than George Lucas ever dreamed of in his unfortunate CGI fantasies. It's all highly enjoyable, and gives one the same giddy, childlike high that Lucas and his oft-accomplice Steven Spielberg specialize in. And yet, one cannot help feeling that something is missing from *Star Trek* in its new, MTV incarnation. The truth is that, for all its fun and games, *Star Trek* is not really a particularly good film.

It is not, however, a particularly bad film either. The visuals are extraordinary, the pace is breakneck, and Leonard Nimoy—whose typecasting in the role of Spock has unfortunately led to him being consistently underrated as an actor—manages to elevate the proceedings a bit, though the rest of the cast, who appear to have been hired mostly because they look like fashion models, is somewhat diminished by his presence. For the most part, however, everything about Abrams's *Star Trek* is mediocre, and not merely by the standards of *Star Trek*—which, despite its classic status, was usually mediocre—but by any standard.

The characters, for instance, appear to have been generated by a cliché machine: Here is the young Captain Kirk as a traumatized, fatherless rebel who secretly longs for heroism. Here he is making an idiot of himself in public. Here is the sage father figure Kirk never had, who sees in him what no one else does, and challenges him to fulfill his potential. Here is Kirk fulfilling that potential by turning his rebelliousness to his advantage. Here he is faced with a crisis situation in which he must take command and show his true character. And here he is in a billion other Hollywood blockbuster movies.

It is not only the Kirk character who seems to have been written by filling in the blanks provided by one of Hollywood's innumerable screenwriting seminar gurus, every other character appears to have been created the same way: There is the repressed overachiever with mommy issues who learns to feel (Spock), the seemingly incompetent sidekick who surprises the audience with his unexpected skill at hand-to-hand combat (Sulu), the foreign accented comic relief (Scotty), the gorgeous and talented Girl Friday who, for some unknown reason, falls for the class freak (Uhura), and so on. Of course, there is also the ugly, deformed villain, whose name is an ironic historical reference (here, it is to the Roman emperor Nero), and is hell bent on revenge as well as plotting to destroy the earth. In this case, *Star Trek* even manages to cannibalize itself. Nero is so faithfully cut and pasted from *The Wrath of Khan* (as Khan himself was cut and pasted, rather heavy-handedly, from *Moby-Dick*) that the two villains even use the same brain-eating space cockroach to torture their prisoners.

This studied lack of any originality whatsoever is, of course, somewhat compensated for by Hollywood's always impressive capacity to simulate the destruction of large objects. Everything, at one point or another, blows up in this movie, and thank God for that, because without such aesthetically pleasing explosions, Star Trek would be essentially unwatchable. It is to the credit of Hollywood's unsung computer nerds that, if the film is anything at all, it is compulsively watchable. But no amount of explosions, however beautifully rendered, can make a great movie.

Of course, no one involved in *Star Trek* actually set out to make a great movie. They set out to make a movie that would make enormous amounts of money, and they have certainly succeeded. This, in and of itself, is not a problem. The *Star Trek* franchise only survives, after all, because it is a cash cow with a massive built-in fan base. How they did it, however, is a bit distressing, not so much because it is unfaithful to the *Star Trek* universe—about which most of us could care less—but because it is so unremittingly and unapologetically juvenile.

If *Star Trek* ever had anything going for it—and this is likely the reason for its continued appeal—it is that the series was, in a certain sense, adult. At the very least, and unlike most products of American pop culture, it did occasionally wander into post-adolescent realms. With all of their drawbacks, the series and its spinoffs did harbor the ambition of being at least slightly more than just another sci-fi adventure. The various true believers who think the series constitutes some profound philosophical statement about the human race are, of course, deluded, and to approach any television series as thought it were a sacred text certainly bespeaks some measure of personal dysfunction; but there is no question that by the terms of most American television and pop cinema, *Star Trek* did aim at least slightly higher than the rest, and occasionally managed to actually hit its target. *Star Trek: The Motion Picture*, for instance, which despite its lousy reputation is probably the best of the films, contains a few genuinely moving moments in between the sci-fi technobabble, and at least tries to say something, however pretentious and clumsily handled.

Abrams's *Star Trek* contains nothing even remotely like this. It is, indisputably, just another sci-fi adventure. Its only ambition—and it makes no bones about it—is to give us all a marvelous rollercoaster ride and send us home blissfully empty-headed. There is nothing inherently wrong with this, but there is nothing particularly extraordinary about it either. It is the kind of thing Jerry Bruckheimer can do in his sleep, and it is clearly what most of the film-going audience desires. But it is also unmistakably childish. The new *Star Trek*, while eminently enjoyable, does seem to be an indication of the fact that American popular culture can no longer stomach anything that might be beyond the capacities of a twelve-year-old to understand. This ubiquitous immaturity may be fun, but it has its consequences, cultural and otherwise. We all enjoy feeling, briefly, like children again, but when there is nothing else, when even the most innocuous, simple-minded, fumbling attempt at something slightly more than that must be rebooted out of existence in order to retain its popularity, something has clearly been lost. I fear that it may be the essential and often unexpectedly gratifying sense of being an adult.

Originally published on June 2, 2009

The Dillinger Debacle

Review of *Public Enemies*, directed by Michael Mann

Every great director has at least one truly bad film in him, and *Public Enemies* is Michael Mann's. It is not just a failure, but one of those movies in which the gap between its quality and its maker's talent is so immense as to be nearly inexplicable. To be fair, it is possible that my expectations for *Public Enemies*, which chronicles the 1933 FBI manhunt for legendary Midwest bank robber John Dillinger, were unfairly high. But from the man who made *Manhunter*, *Thief*, *Last of the Mohicans*, *Collateral*, and the masterpiece *Heat*, a film this empty, dull, lifeless, and—most shocking of all—crudely made cannot be anything other than a major disappointment. This may not be fair, but it is a fact. We expect bad films from the likes of Brett Ratner. We expect great ones from Michael Mann. Such is the price of genius, and in *Public Enemies*, Mann pays it.

In all fairness, however, it must be admitted that *Public Enemies* is not just Mann's failure. It is also another in a long line of equally inexplicable failures to successfully translate the myth of John Dillinger and his eventual demise to the screen. I use the term inexplicable because if the Dillinger legend is anything, it is unquestionably a great story. It has love, violence, friendship, irony, and death. It has a charismatic antihero and, in the person of straitlaced FBI agent Melvin Purvis, who led the manhunt, the stoic nemesis who eventually takes him down. It is a quintessentially American story featuring two classic American archetypes—the free-spirited outlaw and the upstanding sheriff—locked in a duel to the death in a world not unlike that of the Western but much more recognizably ours. In other words, it is a story that seems tailor-made for the movies. And yet, Hollywood has proven consistently incapable of doing it justice.

This is not for lack of trying. Almost from the moment he died in a hail of police bullets outside the Biograph Theater in Chicago, Dillinger has been an object of Hollywood's affections. Over half a dozen films have been made about him, with John

Milius's *Dillinger* (1973), produced by legendary B-movie mogul Roger Corman and starring the much-underrated Warren Oates, probably being the best of them, but none have even approached the heights of the great gangster films like *The Godfather* (1972) or *Bonnie and Clyde* (1967). Most of them have been, at best, forgettable. It seems that something about Dillinger and his tale eludes the powers of cinema, and the best retellings of it have been in books like John Toland's fascinating if sometimes inaccurate *The Dillinger Days* (1963).

The reason for this is probably Dillinger himself. Profoundly evil and, by all accounts, profoundly attractive, he is too complicated, schizophrenic, and disturbing a character for any mainstream film to accurately capture. A violent, charming sociopath, Dillinger was a rapist at thirteen, a convict before he reached twenty, and by the time he was finally cornered and killed by the FBI, a murderer many times over who counted several police officers among his victims. If anything distinguished him from his fellow thugs, it was his unnerving self-awareness, coupled with what seemed to be an instinctive understanding of the role that mass media was coming to play in American life. Decades before Charles Manson and O.J. Simpson, Dillinger was the first American criminal who succeeded in turning himself into a cultural icon. Accordingly, he cultivated a Clark Gable-style mustache, went out of his way to charm the press, never missed a chance for a photo opportunity— especially if it made the authorities look foolish—and became a specialist in such baroque gestures as vaulting gracefully over bank counters and refusing to steal money from poor farmers. He understood, probably because he shared it, that particularly American sympathy for outlaws, especially when their efforts are directed at the vast unknowable systems that seem to govern so much of modern American life. And like most sociopaths, he had a keen sense of what people find attractive, and quickly learned how to exploit it to his advantage.

The real skeleton key to the Dillinger legend, however, is probably the fact that while his chosen profession was somewhat unorthodox, he was very, very good at it. Americans have never much sympathized with Balzac's observation that behind every great fortune lies a crime. They love a success story, no matter how tawdry the details (witness the recent sickening genuflection before the memory of the odious Michael Jackson), and Dillinger was unquestionably a success, robbing banks with seeming impunity, eluding the best efforts of law enforcement for months, and escaping from jails advertised as impregnable. For a brief moment, he was rich, good-looking, and famous, which is usually all Americans need to at least grudgingly admire someone. In this sense, he anticipated modern American icons like Simpson and Jackson, whose transgressions, however horrendous, are endlessly forgiven in the name of their celebrity.

The Dillinger of *Public Enemies* is both much more likable and far less interesting than the original. Played by perennial teen heartthrob Johnny Depp, he is both dull and a pretty nice guy, of which Dillinger was most certainly neither. Depp channels none of the sociopathic joie de vivre which so endeared the outlaw to a bruised and cynical American public. Instead, he remakes the outlaw as a sort of emasculated Byronic hero. Sensitive, sentimental, damaged, and driven, this Dillinger rarely speaks above a monotone, and seems more like a shuffling, drug-addled rock star than a gangster. All of the outlaw's most legendary moments—jumping over the bank counters, letting the farmer keep his money, joking with the press, having his picture taken with his arm on the shoulder of his prosecutor—are portrayed in the film, but Depp's performance is so woefully blank and uninflected that they pass by with barely any impact. While Mann has often used understated, affectless performances to his advantage (witness Robert DeNiro's tour de force of underacting in *Heat*), in this case it serves only to empty Dillinger of what made him interesting in the first place.

Christian Bale's vacant portrayal of Dillinger's pursuer Melvin Purvis is equally woeful. Purvis has generally been portrayed by historians as either a stalwart lawman or a bumbling incompetent, and Mann tries to provide us with a little of both, resulting in a character who is both totally incoherent and just as uninteresting as his quarry. As with Mann's portrayal of Dillinger, the reality was far more compelling and far more disturbing: Purvis was a puritanistic southerner who got the credit for killing Dillinger, though historians now believe there is a strong chance he never fired a shot (Mann's version of events implies that this was in fact the case, though the climactic scene is so bizarrely edited that it is almost impossible to tell who is firing at who). Some thirty years later, the ex-lawman committed suicide, supposedly using the same gun with which he may or may not have shot Dillinger. The conflicting forces that must have been at work in the psyche of such a man ought to make for great drama, perhaps even great tragedy, but Mann more or less ignores them, and by the end of the movie one is simply left wondering what Purvis is doing in the film in the first place.

The only truly persuasive performance in the film belongs to French actress Marion Cotillard, who plays the ostensible love of Dillinger's life, Billie Frechette. Cotillard depicts her as an innocent in love, which is probably inaccurate (before she hooked up with Dillinger, Frechette had already married and left another convicted criminal), but nonetheless touching, and at certain points she displays a ferocious carnality sadly lacking in the portrayal of Dillinger himself. She alone seems to be alive in the way legend demands. Billy Crudup, who plays J. Edgar Hoover, is also effective, though his character rarely rises above the shallow caricature which has become the standard Hollywood portrayal of the late FBI director. Nonetheless, there is an eccentric ruthlessness to Crudup's Hoover that locks him immediately into the mind of the viewer, which cannot be said for the ciphers portrayed by Depp and Bale.

The acting, however, is the least of the film's problems. Most troubling of all, especially for those familiar with Mann's earlier work, is the cinematography, which must be one of the most wrongheaded stylistic decisions in cinema history. Put simply, *Public Enemies* is the ugliest big budget movie ever made. Mann shot the film on high definition video, and while films like the last two *Star Wars* prequels and *Superman Returns* have managed to get a reasonably film-like look out of digital cameras, Mann seems to have opted for a more primitive version of the technology, perhaps in imitation of the execrable Lars Von Trier's equally execrable Dogma movement. The result simply bears out Roman Polanski's opinion that Dogma films look like the cameraman is masturbating while stricken with Parkinson's disease. The images have no depth, movement tends to blur in confusing and disorientating ways, even the night scenes feel overlit, and there are endless shaky-cam shots, every one of which ought to have been filmed on a dolly track. The final effect is to induce nausea in the viewer, and total incomprehension as to why Mann would lavish such expense on costumes, production design, and period detail only to photograph them as if he were making a 1970s no-budget BBC drama.

This becomes even more baffling when one considers Mann's previous work. A notorious perfectionist with a fetish for architectural compositions and modernist styles, the crowning glory of most of his films is their visual beauty, which together with his use of ambient music draws the viewer into that vicarious fugue state which always constitutes cinema at its best. The opening shot of *Heat*, for example, features an LA commuter train slowly approaching the camera as it pulls into an enormous modernist train station, the train's gleaming exterior echoing the architecture surrounding it, so they both appear to become part of the same metallic topography. Throughout the shot, a single ominous note plays on the soundtrack. The viewer has no idea where the film is set or what is happening at this point, but by the time Robert DeNiro steps off the train Mann has us in his pocket. We are all asking ourselves: Who is this man? Why are we watching him? What is about to happen? This is pure filmmaking, holding the viewer spellbound with nothing more than cinema's own wordless, hieroglyphic language.

The worst sin of *Public Enemies*, however, is that it not only fails as cinema but, in making itself unwatchably ugly, actually seems to be at war with it. Whatever his motivations might be—and I suspect Hollywood's fetish for digital technology is one of them— Mann appears to have been stricken with a violent hatred of his own medium. This may eventually lead to something of value, but if Mann continues in this vein, there is a strong chance that we will have to evaluate his career as that of wayward master whose ultimate contribution was, sadly, to the degradation of cinema itself.

Originally published on July 19, 2009

Polanski and the Necessity of Evil

The news of filmmaker Roman Polanski's arrest in Switzerland on an international warrant has, for me and a great many others, reignited an old dilemma, probably unresolvable, regarding art and artists: Namely, the indisputable fact that those who create great work are often not great, or even good people. There is no disputing the fact that Polanski is one of the great filmmakers of the post-war era; *Knife in the Water, Repulsion, Rosemary's Baby, Macbeth, Chinatown, The Tenant, Tess, Bitter Moon, Death and the Maiden,* and *The Pianist* are testimony enough for that. There is also no disputing the fact that 31 years ago he drugged and raped a 13-year-old girl and then fled the United States to France rather than face the possibility of a lengthy prison sentence. Until now, it has been mostly assumed that Polanski would live out the rest of his life in Europe, safe from American justice and free to rehabilitate himself – as he has quite successfully done – as a revered elder statesman of cinema.

Polanski's unexpected arrest has occasioned consternation on both sides of the Atlantic. French government ministers are up in arms, claiming that the long arm of American jurisprudence has maliciously seized one of their national treasures. Poland, which was home to Polanski for most of his youth and early adulthood, is equally outraged. These official voices have been joined by filmmakers and artists from around the world, as well as a few media outlets, who have protested both Polanski's arrest and the manner in which it was accomplished.

Given that Polanski has long since admitted guilt (though he has never really acknowledged wrongdoing) his defenders have generally turned to mitigating circumstances in order to make their case; and it must be admitted that there are a few. Polanski has led, in many ways, a hellish life. As a child, he survived the Nazi occupation of Poland by living as a street urchin in the Krakow ghetto. Once liberated, he was nearly beaten to death by a local psychopath who wanted to steal his bicycle. He watched his family destroyed twice over by mass-murdering lunatics, first Hitler and then Charles

Manson. Any one of these psychological shocks would have been enough to send most people around the bend, or at the very least into serious therapy. It is also true that Polanski did not use physical violence to coerce his victim, that he did serve some prison time for the offense, and that there was more than a bit of misconduct on the part of the presiding judge. Even the prosecutors have admitted that the case was mishandled. And, of course, Polanski's defenders have a bit of a trump card in the fact that his victim has publicly forgiven him.

I cannot shake the suspicion, however, that lurking behind all of these various excuses is the fact that Polanski is a great artist. It is decidedly doubtful that so many in Europe and elsewhere would be outraged if a factory worker, office manager, or Catholic priest, for that matter, were finally caught after so many years evading justice for statutory rape. It is much more likely that they would be outraged at the authorities for taking so long to get around to arresting the perpetrator. The simple truth is that many people—and I freely admit to being one of them—very much wish that Polanski had not done what he did, and are sorely tempted to pretend that, somehow, he didn't. Since we cannot deny the facts, we deny, in some way, his culpability; or, we tell ourselves that, in the end, all things considered, all things being equal, etc., it really wasn't such a big deal. And we do this, I think, for one reason only: We love his movies.

It requires a great deal of effort in the face of this to remind oneself that perhaps the foremost reason people get things wrong is wishful thinking. By and large, we do not listen to what we don't want to hear. Indeed, it is not easy for lovers of cinema, and especially Polanski's cinema, to be honest with ourselves and admit that the only really important question to ask about the Polanski case is this: Did he do it? There is no question that he did. This in turn demands that we ask ourselves whether we think that having sex with a 13 year old girl is acceptable. And there is another question that plagues us—or, at least, it plagues me—*do we really think she was the only one?* Given Polanski's admitted preference for very young women and the Hollywood zeitgeist of the 1970s, it seems sadly doubtful. If we answer no to both of these questions, as most of us will, then we must also force ourselves to recall something else: That producing great work does not constitute a perpetual indulgence. Bob Dylan once said, "Just because you like my stuff doesn't mean I owe you anything." This is true, but it cuts both ways. The artist owes no indulgences to the public; but the public also owes no indulgences to the artist, however brilliant he may be.

In the end, however, I fear this may not be enough. I have a vague suspicion—perhaps an unprovable conviction—that those of us who feel pangs of sympathy for Polanski may be suffering from something a bit more disturbing than mere wishful thinking. I do not put myself on Polanski's level, but the truth is that most of us who write, paint, make films, or engage in some other aesthetic endeavor in order to make some kind of a living, are at least vaguely aware of the fact that great work requires some measure of evil. This does not mean crime or vice; but rather the kind of evil French critic Georges Bataille was alluding to when he wrote, "literature must plead guilty." Great work, he claimed, requires a kind of excess – excess of passion, excess of rationality, excess of religiosity, excess of atheism, excess of morality, excess of immorality – which inevitably transgresses the golden mean that is the most basic ordering factor of society. Bataille was thinking of writers like Blake and Sade; but he could easily have been talking about Polanski, or any of us. Many artists manage to contain this tendency to their work; abiding, perhaps, by Flaubert's dictum that one should be regular and orderly in one's life so as to be violent and original in one's work. Many artists, however, and Polanski is clearly one of them, cannot.

Most of us would like to find some way to forgive him for that. Perhaps because, if only on a subconscious level, we see a bit of ourselves in him and his transgressions; and feel that, in accusing him, we are in some way also accusing ourselves. And perhaps we cover this up with all manner of various remonstrations because we are more keenly aware than most that, as one of Polanski's own characters put it in *Chinatown*, "Most people never have to face the fact that at the right time and place, they're capable of *anything*." To think this way, however, would be the easy way out. It is to mistake the evil that makes for great art with the evil that violates children. They are not the same. It *is* possible to be violent and original in one's work and regular and orderly in one's life. This fact alone demands that the artist, *any* artist, live up to a responsibility that is in some ways more onerous than others. In a sense, the fact that Polanski is a great artist only indicts him further. Those who make their living by acknowledging and exploiting their own capacities for evil ought to be the most careful in preventing it from bleeding out of their work and into their lives; if only because, when they fail to do so, there are so many in high and low places willing to forsake both reason and basic human decency in order to absolve them of it.

Originally published on September 30, 2009

The Slumming Genius

Review of *Shutter Island*, directed by Martin Scorsese

Roughly five minutes into *Shutter Island*, I knew more or less how it would end. For a film that invests another two hours and fifteen minutes in building to an ostensibly shocking twist ending, this is not a particularly good thing. All the more so when the film in question is the work of someone who many cinephiles (and I count myself one of them) consider to be the world's greatest living filmmaker. *Shutter Island* is most certainly not a bad film, but from the likes of Martin Scorsese, it cannot be considered anything other than a disappointment.

One could argue, of course, that we should simply be grateful to see another Scorsese film at all. In an era when most of his contemporaries from the 1970s New Hollywood era have either burned out (William Friedkin, Peter Bogdonavich), died (Robert Altman), or retreated into comfortable mediocrity (Steven Spielberg, George Lucas), the fact that Scorsese is still making films, and still making them with something like the uncompromising intensity of his youth, often seems like reason enough to be indulgent.

Indeed, now that he has been canonized, it is easy to forget that twenty years ago Scorsese seemed to be finished as a major filmmaker. Until his 1990 comeback with *Goodfellas*, a film so ferocious that it almost leaps off the screen and attacks the viewer, Scorsese had meandered through much of the previous decade, apparently lost in a Hollywood that had turned to the blockbuster opening weekend and the high concept event picture as the answer to its post-television malaise. In a cinema that had come to be defined by films like *Star Wars*, Scorsese's raw, violent, low-tech realist style and his desperate, tortured, sometimes psychotic characters appeared to have no place.

Post-*Goodfellas*, however, having not only survived but established himself as a veritable living legend, Scorsese has come to represent a great deal more than his individual films. He is a symbol –

especially to film critics – of a type of filmmaking which, to a great extent, no longer exists today, although a great many of us sorely wish it did. This may go some way toward explaining the unique attitude of most film critics towards his recent work, which has largely been one of gentle indulgence. For the most part, they have been kind, while quietly noting that Scorsese's later films are not quite of the same iconic quality as *Mean Streets*, *Raging Bull*, *Taxi Driver*, and even *Goodfellas*. Even Scorsese's best director Oscar for *The Departed* was greeted with a certain temperance, with many noting that it was more of a lifetime achievement award than anything else.

To a great extent this is an unfortunate state of affairs, because it both underrates much of Scorsese's recent work and ignores his occasional failures. There is no doubt that films such as *The Age of Innocence*, *Kundun*, and *Bringing Out the Dead*, while they have their moments, pale next to the director's previous masterpieces. At the same time, however, the last two decades have produced films like *Casino*, *Gangs of New York*, and *The Departed*, which are not merely great films, but often display a side of Scorsese that does not appear in his more celebrated works, deepening his legacy and complicating the conventional assessment of his oeuvre. Most notably, while Scorsese has become more "mainstream" than he was in the past, his films have ironically become darker and bleaker than they were before. For all their brutality and realism, films like *Mean Streets* and *Raging Bull* nonetheless ended with a sense of redemption for their protagonists; perhaps a bitter and difficult one, but redemption nonetheless. Scorsese's more recent films, like *Gangs of New York*, *The Aviator*, *The Departed*, *Casino*, and even *Goodfellas*, end with their characters either dead or trapped in a metaphoric limbo from which, it is hinted, they may never emerge.

The understandable but unfortunate decision to treat Scorsese as an icon rather than a developing filmmaker has not only led critics to ignore some of his later films' virtues; it has also led them to ignore their flaws. This seems particularly glaring in regard to *Shutter Island*, toward which most critics have reacted in the typical fashion, which is something along the lines of "It's great, but not quite as great as…" before proceeding to cite one of the director's 1970s triumphs. The truth, however, is that even viewed in the context of Scorsese's work in the 1990s and 2000s, *Shutter Island* is a major failure.

The film is, as everyone likely knows by now, a thriller; but it is not a particularly good one. The plot, such as it is, is remarkably clichéd: Sometime in the 1950s, federal marshals Teddy Daniels (Leonardo DiCaprio) and his partner Chuck Aule (Mark Ruffalo) are ferried to an isolated island off of Massachusetts which houses a state of the art prison for the criminally insane. A patient has inexplicably gone missing, and Daniels and Aule are charged with finding her. There is no way off the island, a hurricane is bearing down, and as the investigation proceeds, it becomes clear that everything—naturally—is not what it seems. Daniels, who in the finest Scorsese tradition is tortured by traumatic events in his past, quickly becomes convinced that a dark conspiracy is at work. To recount any more of the plot would ruin the film for anyone who has not seen it, but suffice it to say that most of the film's surprisingly long running time is taken up by red herrings, false trails, and the kind of powerhouse set pieces that Scorsese can direct in his sleep. By the time the twist ending—which, as noted above, is obvious almost from the beginning—rolls around, one has the depressing sensation of having watched a master trying his best to keep us all entertained but, in the end, is just going through the motions.

To be fair, this is not entirely Scorsese's fault. The film's story is, to put it bluntly, depressingly generic, and no amount of cinematic pyrotechnics can obscure the fact that, as talented as Scorsese undoubtedly is with the camera, we have seen this story done—usually better—a thousand times before. The film's acting is equally problematic. While there are some good performances, especially from Ben Kingsley as the prison's disconcertingly mild-mannered administrator—and it is always a treat to see Max Von Sydow in anything—Leonardo DiCaprio is simply not capable of the kind of emotional intensity and range required by the film's central character. While his collaboration has been a boon to Scorsese's recent career, allowing the director to command budgets which he could not acquire otherwise, DiCaprio lacks the preternatural talent displayed by the likes of Robert DeNiro and Daniel Day-Lewis, whose work with Scorsese is justifiably legendary. One cannot imagine DiCaprio giving the kind of titanic performance DeNiro delivered in *Raging Bull*, and in *Gangs of New York* he was simply dwarfed by the towering presence of Day-Lewis. *Shutter Island* is, unfortunately, no exception to this, and while DiCaprio does his best to appear sweaty, tortured, traumatized, and driven, his performance is ultimately a shallow one, never shedding the pretty-boy immaturity which has haunted DiCaprio's work from the beginning.

Nonetheless, this is a Martin Scorsese picture, and any director as obsessively fixated on his work as he reportedly is must ultimately bear the blame for his failures. In some ways, however, this failure is not surprising. Despite his undeniable brilliance, Scorsese is not particularly good at making thrillers or at making genre films in general. His greatest talent has always been for human drama, and once hemmed in by the rules and regs of a particular genre, his talent often seems to become mechanical and soulless. Even his celebrated gangster films are more about character and sociological observation than adhering to the formal mores of the genre. His one previous attempt at a thriller, 1991's *Cape Fear*, is an enjoyable but forgettable potboiler, carried mostly by Robert DeNiro's charismatic central performance.

Shutter Island is even more obviously a case of Scorsese being out of his natural element. While the visuals are flawless and the director seems to have packed the film with homages to every thriller ever made, this ultimately leaves the viewer unmoved. While watching it, one cannot help feeling that we have seen this film before—and better—at the hands of Mario Bava, Dario Argento, Alfred Hitchcock, Roman Polanski, Roger Corman, and no doubt many others older and more obscure who Scorsese has excavated from his reportedly encyclopedic knowledge of cinema. But homage is not by definition interesting, and ultimately *Shutter Island* feels like a shallow and pointless exercise; the work of a slumming genius who is capable, and must know he is capable, of a great deal more.

Originally published on March 18, 2010

The Most Righteous Gentile

Review of *Inglourious Basterds*, directed by Quentin Tarantino

My first experience with Quentin Tarantino came in at the age of fourteen, when I attended an advance showing of *Reservoir Dogs* at the Boston Film Festival. Half the audience walked out during the notorious ear scene, and my father—who had to accompany me, because Boston, in all its puritanism, is one of the few cities that actually does care if under-17s see rated-R movies—swore that he would never take me to another film again. I wonder what my father, who once told me he joined the US Army so that if the Nazis came back they'd only get one shot at him, would say about Tarantino now; given that his new film, *Inglourious Basterds*, ends with a Jewish-American soldier blasting Hitler's face to pieces with a machine gun.

I am not sure I know what to think about Tarantino now, given that he has somehow emerged as the most righteous cinematic gentile since Otto Preminger. With *Inglourious Basterds*, which chronicles an alternate history of World War II in which a Jewish girl out for revenge and a group of Jewish-American partisans led by a bloodthirsty Tennessean (the eponymous Basterds) end the conflict by blasting, burning, stabbing, clubbing, and shooting the Nazi high command to smithereens, Tarantino has transformed himself into the avatar of Jewish dreams of impossible vengeance. The director not only does not deny this, but actively endorses the idea, claiming that his film is a healthy antidote to more standard depictions of the Holocaust like *Schindler's List*, in which the Jews are routinely portrayed as helpless victims. Even more to the point, Tarantino—while he has not actually come out and said as much—appears to be aware of the fact that no Jewish director could have made a film as unapologetically brutal as *Inglourious Basterds*. It is true that most Jews dream, at one point or another, of killing Nazis, and certainly of killing Hitler; but the idea of slaughtering one's enemies without guilt, doubt, or regret is a place most Jews still are not comfortable going, as a cursory comparison between Tarantino's gleefully murderous new film and Steven Spielberg's lugubrious *Munich* amply demonstrates. Most Jews today, especially in America, prefer to think of the prophet Isaiah's admonition to beat one's swords into plowshares, rather than Joel's rejoinder, "Beat your plowshares into swords and your pruning hooks into spears. Let the weak rise and say, I am strong."

Tarantino is unquestionably a man who likes pushing people's buttons, and he's pushing them now in a way he never has before. I don't what the effect of *Inglourious Basterds* is on a gentile audiences, but if the reaction of its Jewish attendees is anything to go by, it is certainly forcing many Jews to sometimes squirmingly acknowledge the fact that they rather enjoy the idea of bashing in a Nazi's skull with a baseball bat. Tarantino seems to know, or to have instinctively guessed, that many, perhaps most, Jews in the post-Holocaust era see themselves as having made an unspoken pact with the non-Jewish world: They will serve as the living symbol of the victims of man's inhumanity to man, and in return they agree to suppress their eminently natural desire to do as the Basterds do to those who committed the inhumanity in question. Tarantino appears to enjoy the possibility of blasting this comfortable delusion wide open, which may be why the film has been marketed as something like a cross between *The Chosen* and *Rambo*.

The only problem with this is that the film itself is not as advertised. Far from a rollicking piece of non-stop Nazi-slaughtering action, *Inglourious Basterds* is surprisingly slow and dialogue heavy. The Basterds themselves appear for, at best, half of its two and a half hour running time, and while the film certainly contains moments of Tarantino's signature ultra-violence, most of it consists of people sitting and talking. Sometimes, they talk until something happens; sometimes they just talk. Sometimes its interesting; sometimes it isn't. Some of it runs much too long, some of it much too slow. In the end, the film feels closer to Tarantino's less than successful *Jackie Brown*, which shared the same slow pacing and seemingly episodic storyline, than his more grandiose crowd-pleasers like *Pulp Fiction* and *Kill Bill*. Told in five separate chapters, each of which is essentially a set piece unto itself, the film twists, turns, and tangles into itself along its meandering way toward the inevitable explosive climax.

There is some marvelous stuff strewn along the way. Taken as a whole, the film is less a tale of Jewish revenge than a grand homage to Tarantino's favorite war movies, from *The Big Red One* to *Patton* and *The Dirty Dozen* via Sergio Leone and a thousand B-movies, laced with a morbid fascination with Nazi propaganda films. There is no doubt that Tarantino's talent for cherry-picking moments from other movies and rearranging them into a self-referential but also deconstructive collage, drawing the viewer wholly into his world, has not diminished. Indeed, by the time David Bowie comes thudding on to the soundtrack in all his 1980s synth-driven glory, it fits so perfectly into Tarantino's pastiche that one barely notices the anachronism.

Unfortunately, there is also a great deal in *Inglourious Basterds* that simply does not work. In particular, the casting is surprisingly weak; especially for Tarantino, who can usually be counted on to provide at least one or two great performances. Brad Pitt's over-the-top commander of the Basterds, half back country hick and half George S. Patton, is fun to watch, and the other Basterds at least look the part, but none of them have the requisite charisma to stand out in roles which are more about presence than character. Melanie Laurent is mostly maudlin as the orphaned Jewish avenger who finds herself running a Paris cinematheque in which the Nazi high command is a bit too serendipitously gathered. While she manages one great line, "This is the face of Jewish vengeance!" for the most part she sits around looking depressed. The film's most charismatic performance belongs, as it usually does, to the villain. In this case it is Christoph Waltz as the sadistic but brilliant SS officer Hans Landa. Waltz chews so much scenery that he quickly becomes the film's most dominating presence, which is mostly to the detriment of the movie as a whole. The film's best performance, ironically, probably belongs to Mike Myers, who has a brilliant camp turn as the quintessential stiff-upper-lip, stick-up-his-ass British army officer.

More than anything else, however, *Inglourious Basterds* feels over-cooked. Tarantino reportedly worked on the film for over a decade in one form or another, and the final product smacks of something which has been too much pondered over. It plays as an over-calculated and oddly bloodless piece, as if its original inspiration had been slowly leached out over time. Several of its set pieces, especially a lengthy sequence in a pub played almost entirely in German (which could easily have been cut down by half), are uneven, repetitious, and — a first for Tarantino — somewhat boring. The film certainly has its moments, and a few of them are great ones. But on the whole, one feels that Tarantino loved his film too well. Orson Welles once said that the most important lesson for a director to learn is how to walk away from something. In this case, Tarantino, apparently, couldn't.

Ultimately, the quality of *Inglourious Basterds* as a film may be largely irrelevant. The buttons it pushes have been waiting to be pushed for a long time; and personally, I can't be anything but bemused that Tarantino, of all people, has been the one to push them. Nonetheless, there is now at least the possibility that, thanks to him, Jewish filmmakers may finally be able to admit that they do not have to portray themselves as more than human out of the fear that others will see them as less than human. As a movie, *Inglourious Basterds* leaves much to be desired; as a pop cultural event, it is a unique and, I think, rather welcome transgression.

Originally published on September 25, 2009

The Lost World of the Watchmen

Review of *Watchmen*, directed by Zack Snyder

Watching Zack Snyder's new adaptation of the happily uncredited Alan Moore and the very-much credited Dave Gibbons's *Watchmen* is somewhat like watching the CliffsNotes to *Moby Dick*. Regarding any other product of the comics medium, such a statement would be ludicrously pretentious. In the case of *Watchmen*, however, we are dealing with something very much like a great work, and films of great works are rarely successful. Made under conditions of extreme aesthetic intimidation, they are always caught between the desire to capture the success of the original by osmosis, i.e. imitation, and the knowledge that cinematic adaptations are almost always at their best when they are least faithful. Snyder's *Watchmen*, unfortunately, tends to have the worst of both worlds. Its faithfulness undermines its power, and the moments when it is unfaithful are rarely an improvement.

Snyder has what many other filmmakers in his position have lacked, however, namely a good excuse. *Watchmen* has long been acknowledged—by director Terry Gilliam and Moore himself, amongst others—to be essentially unfilmable. Its plot can be described fairly simply: a group of retired superheroes, most of whom have no super powers, try to solve the murder of a former colleague in an alternative 1985, in which the world is poised on the brink of nuclear annihilation. This brief if accurate description fails to convey, however, anything of the intensity with which *Watchmen* assaults the reader. Dense, non-linear, and kaleidoscopic in structure, *Watchmen* is a book which defies and defines its genre while simultaneously deconstructing it. The comparison to *Moby Dick* is apt in that *Watchmen*'s power derives from the fact that it remains a genre piece even while it is subjected to an overwhelming concentration of forces which lead, ultimately, to the sublime destruction of itself and its own medium. Much as Melville set out to write a simple, above-average tale of adventure on the high seas, and ended up anticipating literary modernism by over half a century, Moore and Gibbons set out to create an interesting twist on the superhero genre, and ended up producing a tour de force of post-modernism. *Watchmen* is a book that got away from its authors and inadvertently became more than the sum of its many, many parts.

Snyder's film, unfortunately, is nothing but parts. One senses while watching it that the filmmakers cherry-picked the book for its most impressive setpieces, which they then quite faithfully, and quite spectacularly, committed to film, sometimes almost frame-for-frame. Certainly, this leads to some extraordinary moments, but they remain only moments. In Moore's book, by contrast, they lead inexorably, but completely without the reader's awareness, to a stunning final reveal in which all the loose threads, all the bizarre twists and turns of his seemingly inscrutable narrative come together in a single, apocalyptic moment involving a *vagina dentata* straight out of a Freudian nightmare. This horror has, notoriously, been erased from Snyder's film, along with most of the other small details which could not have been contained in a movie of any manageable length, but which are essential to Moore's steady escalation toward something like the end of the world. Without its great magician's reveal, and everything that leads up to it, *Watchmen* on film feels somehow partial, unfinished, and lost in its own web of homages to the formidable original.

This is not to say, however, that the film is wholly without its virtues. Ironically, most of its best moments are those which are least faithful, such as the film's opening credits, in which a hilarious montage of setpieces rewrites the history of the late 20th century to the tune of Bob Dylan's "Times They Are A-Changin'". One wonders if Snyder's *Watchmen* might have been far better had it been less reverent or, at least, if it had been less reverent in the right places.

The soundtrack is also unquestionably a strong point. Echoing the innumerable irreverent references to pop culture which fill Moore's original, the film manages to interweave Dylan, 80s pop, Wagner, shrieking punk rock, Simon and Garfunkel, Philip Glass, Nat King Cole, Mozart's "Requiem," and, in a garishly funny sex scene, Leonard Cohen's original "Hallelujah" – which may finally take its rightful place above the seemingly endless parade of inferior cover versions – into a vertiginous mosaic which, while mostly unrelated to the original book, nonetheless successfully echoes its kaleidoscopic style.

This, unfortunately, is one of the film's few outright successes. Snyder's preference for fast editing and *Matrix*-style camerawork does not lend much to Moore's intricate and surprisingly slow-paced narrative, and the acting is almost universally maudlin. The lone standout is Jackie Earle Haley as the semi-psychotic vigilante Rorschach, whose propensity for cathartic violence is matched only by his stalwart sense of absolute justice. Haley is so good, oscillating between ominous calm and manic insanity without ever descending into camp, that he almost makes the viewer forget Matthew Goode as the preternatural genius Ozymandias, who is so badly miscast that his performance, through no real fault of his own, almost completely destroys the film.

The greatest failure of *Watchmen*, however, may be simply a matter of timing. Love it or hate it, Snyder's previous film *300* touched the zeitgeist in a way that could not have been premeditated beforehand. In the world we live in today, the story of a desperate battle between a society based on religious tyranny and one struggling toward reason and freedom cannot help but touch the deepest recesses of our collective unconscious. *Watchmen*, on the other hand, as both a book and a film, is a commentary on a world that is now past: the world of the Cold War, brinkmanship in Afghanistan, and the threat of nuclear war between the superpowers. The nuclear threat has not gone away, but the suitcase bomb is now a far more terrifyingly immediate prospect than the ICBM. *300* was the right film at the right time, *Watchmen*, whatever its quality, is the wrong film for the wrong time.

In all fairness, this is not really Snyder's fault. If his film is, in a sense, dated, it is only because its source material is now also dated, and not merely in terms of politics and history. The Achilles heel of deconstruction is that it can only be done once. Today, *Watchmen* can be read with simple admiration for its skill and quality. When it first appeared, however, it was groundbreaking in a way that it cannot be now. In essence, Moore created a superhero tale about the impossibility of doing right. At the time, this was a watershed. But the superhero has caught up with Moore and normalized his vision.

Along with the USSR, nuclear war, and a perpetual Nixon presidency, the idea of the compromised superhero has lost its sting. We have grown used to compromised heroes in a compromised world. Where *Watchmen*'s tortured, neurotic, sometimes mad crusaders were once a daring subversion of genre conventions, they have now become a genre convention, and have thus been rendered somewhat banal. The impossibility of doing right is no longer much of a revelation. In the end, Snyder's film may be a failure only because it is a transgression thrown into an era in which transgression no longer exists.

Originally published on March 14, 2009

Kill All the Humans

Review of *Avatar*, directed by James Cameron

I resisted seeing *Avatar* for as long as humanly possible, as much out of sheer contrarianism as anything else, but ultimately I too succumbed to the phenomenon, and got my eyeful of James Cameron's latest mega-blockbuster, now the highest-grossing film of all time.

Cameron, I must confess, is one of those directors I have never known quite what to do with. His technique is impeccable; his technological innovations known to all; and his capacity for tapping into the collective cinematic unconscious, somehow knowing what people want to see before they do, undeniable. And yet, I have always felt that there is something missing from Cameron's films. He is a Spielberg without the sense of wonder; Kubrick without the burning, uncompromising intelligence; Scorsese without the pervasive sense of Catholic pity. Often, he seems to be a mere sketch of a great director, calculating, obsessive, utterly in control, and yet oddly and persistently empty.

Avatar, it must be admitted, is no exception to this. Everything its admirers and its detractors have said about it is more or less true. The visuals are extraordinary, the action scenes stunning, the special effects flawless, and the pure splendor of it all at times transporting. At the same time, the story is absurdly derivative, the characters stick figures at best, the dialogue lamentable, and its politics painfully didactic. There is no doubt that it is enormously effective on its own terms, but one cannot help feeling that everything about it except its special effects is oddly cursory and even amateurish.

The plot is, of course, well known to everyone by now, and hardly bears much recounting. Sometime in the future, a mining corporation on the distant planet Pandora finds itself in conflict with the humanoid natives, the Na'avi. Earth, it seems, is slowly becoming uninhabitable due to some series of unknown, though one presumes environmental, disasters; and it is much in need of Pandora's most precious resource, referred to, stupefyingly, as "unobtainium." Early attempts at reconciliation between human and Na'avi have produced the Avatar program, in which the minds of human beings are transferred into genetically engineered Na'avi bodies. Whatever *modus vivendi* once existed with the natives, however, is about to fall apart, and a wounded marine named Jake (Sam Worthington) is made an Avatar for the purposes of intelligence gathering soon to lead to military action against the Na'avi. As anyone who has seen *Dances With Wolves* could have predicted, Jake finds himself enthralled with the Na'avi and their nature-worshipping culture, falls in love with a native princess (Zoe Saldana), and ends up leading the natives into a victorious war against the human interlopers.

Clearly, Cameron intended all this as some sort of vicarious revenge fantasy, predicated on the noble savage fetish shared by many in the developed world and the director's own palpable—and palpably ironic—technophobia. Indeed, no film in recent memory has sold itself so intensely on the basis of its technological innovations while proffering its audience such an intensely anti-technological message. This message has, of course, been the defining obsession of Cameron's career. *The Terminator* is based on the idea of sentient machines rising up against their creators, *Aliens* depicts its technologically advanced but all too human characters overwhelmed by their purely organic enemies, *The Abyss* offers up both environmentalist and anti-nuclear sentiment in spades, and *Titanic* adopts for itself the 20th century's most famous metaphor for man's technological arrogance and resulting comeuppance.

In a certain sense, the obvious contradiction at the heart of Cameron's work and its creator—a technophobic gearhead, of all things—is what has kept them both somewhat interesting. It cannot be denied that Cameron has had a very long and very successful career in a notoriously fickle occupation. He has, after all, directed the two highest-grossing films of all time twice in a row. Obviously, there is a large audience for the type of paradox Cameron personifies.

This should not necessarily be surprising. One of the defining aspects of psychological life in the developed world, especially in the aftermath of the gas chamber and the atomic bomb, has been a love of the ease and convenience that technology offers coupled with an equally intense fear of its power and essential unknowability. Most of us have no idea how an electric light bulb actually works, but we know that once the sun goes down the world is noticeably more threatening without it. Our knowledge of both our own ignorance and our own dependence on technology cannot help but create an inner tension that Cameron clearly shares and expresses with all the verve and aplomb of DeMille and his fellow masters of Hollywood spectacle.

Nonetheless, one cannot help but note a certain disturbing progression in Cameron's work: At the end of the *Terminator* films he personally directed, mankind seems to have averted the machine uprising that set the initial plot in motion; at the end of *The Abyss*, the undersea aliens decide not to annihilate mankind in a series of environmental disasters; at the end of *Titanic*, love conquers all, even death and eternity. At the end of *Avatar*, however, we are rather summarily informed that, following the victory of the Na'avi, the humans have been "sent back to their dying world." No indication is given that humanity will be capable of surviving back on Earth, and the film does not seem overly concerned with the question. The implications of this are fairly obvious, and for anyone who has seen Cameron's previous films, inevitable: The annihilation of the human race.

The moment passes so quickly that a great many viewers might well miss its significance, but it seems to be both essential to Cameron's fantasy (which is, after all, a fantasy of revenge) and the inevitable culmination of his worldview, which both fetishizes and demonizes technology while painting an idealized and wholly unrealistic picture of the natural world. It is no secret that people who inordinately love machines tend not to care very much for human beings, and the same goes for those who inordinately love trees. There seems to be some paradoxical meeting place between the idolatry of the natural and the idolatry of the artificial. What it results in is not unprecedented, though it is bizarre, and unquestionably new. There are many, after all, who hate themselves, hate other people, hate their country, hate their occupation, or simply hate with no particular object in mind. What *Avatar* presents us, however, is

36

someone who quite simply hates his own species. Misanthropy is not new either, but to see it emerge on a purely scientific and materialist basis is certainly something unique to our era. What we are to make of such a worldview, however, is a question for a later generation; one that, I hope, will survive it.

Originally published on April 20, 2010

The Imaginarist

Review of *The Imaginarium of Doctor Parnassus*, directed by Terry Gilliam

Terry Gilliam, the former member of Monty Python and celebrated filmmaker, now nearing seventy, has spent much of the last few decades fighting a long and, one must admit, bruising battle against the real world. And while he has not always enjoyed success—indeed, he has tasted outright disaster several times—Gilliam has nonetheless earned his place as one of the great cinematic avatars of the imagination. If his return to form with the fascinating, frustrating, utterly original *The Imaginarium of Doctor Parnassus* is anything to go by, the cult of realism has never had a more avowed and passionate enemy.

The imagination is not much in style nowadays, as the fetish of realism appears to have overwhelmed all other styles of filmmaking, bleeding into even such fantastical genres as fantasy and science fiction. The enormous success of Christopher Nolan's rebooted, hyper-realist Batman series is a case in point. While the gritty Batman has enjoyed renewed box office domination, Bryan Singer's attempt at restarting the far more inherently fantastical—that is, imaginative—Superman character was considered an embarrassing failure. Singer's *Superman Returns*, it must be admitted, does suffer from serious flaws, but it is a far better film than it is given credit for, and the real reason behind its relative lack of success would seem to be its utter failure to capture the zeitgeist—the same zeitgeist which propelled Nolan's *The Dark Knight* into the financial stratosphere.

Certainly, films like Peter Jackson's *Lord of the Rings* trilogy and James Cameron's *Avatar* have achieved enormous success by depicting fantastic worlds. Nonetheless, there is an overriding realism to all of them, in the sense that they attempt, through the accumulation of detail and seriousness of purpose, to depict these extraordinary realms as absolutely, essentially *real*. The whole point of the cutting edge special effects these films employ is to succeed in playing this particular trick on the audience. The idea of depicting a realm that is consciously unreal appears to have disappeared almost completely from the cinematic consciousness.

There are, of course, a few exceptions to this: some of the films of David Lynch; Guillermo Del Toro's *Pan's Labyrinth*; even Stanley Kubrick's *Eyes Wide Shut*, which, like the films of Antonioni, appears to be realistic but behaves according to the mores of a dream. The most prominent exception, however, is Terry Gilliam. The imaginative has not only defined his career, but given him a cause, and he often speaks with determination and bitter humor of the constant struggle he undergoes in order to bring his dreams to the screen.

This struggle may be why Gilliam's work occupies such a singular place in the annals of fantastic cinema. Some films are pure realism, some are pure dream, but Gilliam's are about the tension between the two. In all of his best films, the cruel and concrete world presses in on the limitless world of the dream. This appears most famously in his dystopian fantasy *Brazil* (1985), in which a faceless bureaucrat escapes from the oppressive urban tyranny in which he lives by disappearing into his fantasies. *Brazil* is a visually stunning film throughout, but in its dream sequences it becomes truly sublime. The bureaucrat reimagines himself as a winged Icarus pursuing a naked maiden through the sky, until enormous skyscraper-like forms burst up from the ground, blotting out the sun, and he is forced to fight a duel with an enormous samurai that bleeds fire. Anything, it seems, can and does happen within this dream realm—impossible beauty and heroism, love and death, horror and grotesque violence— and these things point to the human possibilities snuffed out by the stultifying, technologically dominated world outside. Of course, there is also the darker side to this coin. All of *Brazil*'s dream sequences are reflections of the oppressive waking world, which in the end conquers and dominates them, leaving the protagonist lost in his own mind while his body remains physically imprisoned. Gilliam's film is ambiguous on the question of whether this constitutes a triumph or a defeat for the imagination, and this ambiguity has persisted throughout his best work.

Perhaps the best example of this is the much-maligned, little-seen, and tragically underrated *The Adventures of Baron*

Munchausen (1988). A financial disaster upon its release, *Munchausen* is perhaps Gillam's purest distillation of the conflict between reality and dream. Trapped in a besieged city, the legendary adventurer and notorious confabulator Baron Munchausen and his intrepid companions set out on a series of fantastical adventures, none of which may actually be happening. They travel to the moon, down to the depths of Hades to meet Vulcan and Venus, and into the belly of a sea monster. After they return to save the day, the entire adventure is revealed to be a tale told by the Baron to an audience in the city theater. "And that," he pronounces, "was only one of the many occasions on which I met my death." The film leaves us with nothing but questions. Was it all a tall tale? Did any of it really happen? Is the Baron alive or dead? Is he the real thing or an impostor? What is certain is that Gilliam cultivates this ambiguity throughout, as well as emphasizing both the infinite possibilities of fantasy and the constant proximity of death – the ultimate expression of reality.

The horrendous commercial failure of *Munchausen* has haunted Gilliam ever since, and as a result he has spent much of the rest of his career flirting uncomfortably with the mainstream. He has met with both success (*Twelve Monkeys*) and failure (*The Brothers Grimm*) in this, and many of these films have managed to embrace Gilliam's favorite theme to a certain extent. In *Fear and Loathing in Las Vegas* (1998), it is drugs that occasion the journey into the fantasy world. In *Tideland* (2005), it is childhood trauma. In *The Fisher King* (1991), it is mental illness. None of these, however, have fully retained the wholly unleashed and wholly original sense of visual phantasmagoria that marked *Brazil* or *Munchausen*. None of them, in other words, have felt as if they emerged fully formed out of Gilliam's dreams.

Based on the little that can be gleaned from the excellent documentary *Lost in La Mancha* (2002), Gilliam's aborted 1999 attempt to film *The Man Who Killed Don Quixote* might have been a step back toward the sensibility that produced his finest work. But we were forced to wait another ten years for Gilliam to return completely to form with *The Imaginarium of Doctor Parnassus*, which is not only based on the conflict between fantasy and reality but takes the idea further than Gilliam has ever done before.

The Imaginarium of Doctor Parnassus is a fantasy that takes place in a very real and ugly world. In a decrepit and commercialized present-day London, a ragtag group of performers arrive in a horse-drawn carriage. They are led by the mysterious Doctor Parnassus (Christopher Plummer), whose seemingly innocuous plastic mirror is actually a doorway into a dream world – the imaginarium. Whoever passes through the mirror is treated to hallucinatory visions of their greatest pleasures, desires, and temptations. Parnassus is haunted, however, by the demonic Mr. Nick (a perfectly cast Tom Waits). Long ago, Parnassus made a dark bargain with Mr. Nick, and the devil has come to collect. Hoping to make good on his debt, Parnassus and his companions place their hopes in Toby (the late Heath Ledger), a smooth-talking huckster who is not all he seems to be.

The film has now become notorious because of Ledger's sudden and unexpected death, and the ingenious method Gilliam devised to complete the film in his absence. Gilliam simply recast the part, so that each time Ledger enters the imaginarium, he is played by a different actor – Johnny Depp, Jude Law, and Colin Farrell, respectively. While it is impossible to know what would have been otherwise, it seems that this necessary piece of stunt casting actually improves the film, because it adds a new dimension to Gilliam's concept of the imagination. In *Parnassus*, the imagination is now a world in which one literally becomes *another person entirely*. And, it is hinted, this may be for both good and ill.

Whereas before, the struggle depicted in Gilliam's films was always between the imaginary and the real; in *Parnassus*, the struggle also takes place within the imaginary world itself. The devil, he seems to say, is always present to tempt the darker side of those who enter the imaginarium; and our inner selves can be just as ugly and oppressive as the world outside. In this, Gilliam appears to be approaching the depth and complexity of his most kindred fellow, the late Frederico Fellini, whose masterpiece *8 ½*, amongst others, depicts its protagonist's fantasy world as both beautiful and fraught with nightmares.

This deeper journey into the realms of the imaginary also appears to have inspired Gilliam to new creative heights. Gilliam has always been known for his extraordinary sense of the visual, but in *Parnassus* he outdoes himself. Some of the visions conjured up by the imaginarium are unforgettable: a lily pad world composed of high-heeled shoes and pearl necklaces, a madcap chase with giant ladders used for locomotion, a massive babushka whose head pops off to reveal Tom Waits inside working the controls screaming "I'm goin' to Chicago, baby!", and in the climactic scene, a world literally cracking to pieces like glass.

It is a fine thing to see Gilliam return to form, but *The Imaginarium of Doctor Parnassus* is even more welcome because it is, at long last, a film that makes no pretense to realism, and which embraces the imagination as not only a legitimate but also a desirable subject for cinema. Such an anomaly ought to be celebrated because, in a sense, the imagination is the only subject of cinema. Even the most realistic film is essentially a fantasy, a theatrical presentation that seeks to emulate and approximate the real, but can never actually *be* real. *Parnassus* reminds us of what cinema really is, and thus what it is capable of being. As Bernardo Bertolucci once put it, seeing a movie is an experience in which "we are all sitting in the amniotic darkness, and we are all dreaming the same dream." Only cinema is capable of creating this kind of communal imagination, and it is often at its best when it acknowledges this fact. At the moment, Terry Gilliam is an outsider in the cinematic world, and he may always remain so. But we ought to hope that his dedication to the imaginative possibilities of cinema may inspire both himself and others to continue their quiet defiance of the cult of realism.

Originally published on July 16, 2010

Down the Rabbit Hole

Review of *Alice in Wonderland*, directed by Tim Burton

One can almost see the meeting of studio executives that preceded the production of Tim Burton's new film of *Alice in Wonderland*. A half dozen cocaine-addled Bard graduates blinking through the aftereffects of yet another night of silicone implanted satyriasis and quietly musing on the possibilities inherent in Lewis Carroll's century-old fairy tale. "What," says one, "if instead of being a little girl, Alice is, like, a hot girl-power feminist teenager?" "Cool!" says another, "and what if like, everything that happened in the book happened, like, *before*." "Yeah!" says another, "and what if, instead of just wandering around seeing weird things, she has to go *Lord of the Rings* on, like, something…?" "Awesome!" says a third, "and what if, like, at the end, the Mad Hatter dances like Michael Jackson? That would be so cool." At this point, someone calls to find out if Johnny Depp is available.

And so it went, one imagines, until the big budget, 3-D, Dolby Sensurround travesty of one of the most beloved pieces of British whimsy literature was completed; leaving the Walt Disney studios a great deal richer and its viewers considerably poorer in every sense of the word.

Indeed, in its own way, *Alice in Wonderland* is a watershed moment: It marks for all time the precise moment in history that Johnny Depp's various star turns as effeminate eccentrics ceased to be amusing and simply became irritating; it marks the collapse of a once great filmmaker into a tired, burned out, used-up husk of an artist spewing out generic blockbusters on command; it marks the terrible denouement of Helena Bonham Carter's decade long meltdown, here immortalized in the form of a screeching woman with a very, very large head; and, of course, it marks the moment that we received the final, incontrovertible proof that Hollywood is run, staffed, maintained, and defended by infantile cretins who are convinced—and judging by the box office returns for this film they are, unfortunately, largely correct—that the rest of us are idiots.

As hinted at above, this new *Alice in Wonderland* has, in fact, very little to do with *Alice in Wonderland*. It goes so far as to change the name of the "Wonderland" in question, so that it is now "Underland," a change which was presumably made for the same reason that the film's young heroine is now considerably older and more violent; namely, the raw unabashed terror of seeming uncool. Practically everything in the film has, in fact, been altered from its source material in the name of this blubbering idolatry of hip. Instead of an innocuous child adrift in a dream world, this Alice is a spunky (of course) and headstrong (naturally) young woman who will not— just *will not*—allow herself to be married to a silly young man just because the mores of her time demand it. (One can almost picture Oprah and her audience of fellow idiots shrieking "you go girl!") Naturally, she does what young women in similar situations have done throughout human history: She chases a cartoon rabbit down a hole, emerges in a depressingly cartoonish computer-generated fantasy world, and goes on a grand quest to kill a large animal.

At this point, one must stop and simply emit a very long and tired sigh; since this is, in fact, some fool's idea of what would make a good film of *Alice in Wonderland*: Turn it into a cross between *Lord of the Rings*, *The Chronicles of Narnia*, and *Who Framed Roger Rabbit?*. To the extent that any remnant of the original remains, it is in the various well known characters who appear in surprisingly bad CGI renderings (they are essentially indistinguishable from cartoons) in order to guide Alice on her quest to kill the large animal in question; which is, of course, the Jabberwocky, chosen, one is forced to conclude, because it is more or less the only character in Lewis Carroll's original menacing enough to serve as a plot point contrived by a mentally-challenged screenwriter solely in order to put a battle scene at the end the movie. This is only a rough sketch of the film's plot, mainly because the film's plot is completely incomprehensible; and as soon as Alice goes down the rabbit hole the film goes with her, and the viewer is left jumping from setpiece to setpiece with little or no explanation, exposition, or, ultimately, interest. There are a handful of amusing moments , mostly at the hands of the Cheshire

Cat, but by the end one is left with the distinct feeling that one has just seen a lousy knockoff of *Return of the King* that was, for some reason, entitled *Alice in Wonderland*.

Even a lousy knockoff of *Return of the King*, however, would probably not include what can only be described as the film's *Plan 9 From Outer Space* moment; a moment so bad, so ill-conceived, so inexplicably wrong in terms of context, style, good taste, and sanity, that it pushes the film out of the realm of mere blockbuster mediocrity and into that infamous stratosphere where the likes of *Gigli*, *Showgirls*, and *Catwoman* reside in the eternal twilight of their own awfulness. It is the moment when Johnny Depp, doing his usual camp as the Mad Hatter, breaks into what can only be described as a cross between a poor imitation of Michael Jackson and an epileptic fit, accompanied — in a film that has had a conventional symphonic score throughout — by what someone apparently thought was a funky R&B backbeat. At this moment, "bad" becomes a mere word, to be replaced in all dictionaries by "*Alice in Wonderland*."

Saddest of all the creatures emerging from the wreckage of this latest testament to Hollywood's utter vacuity, calculated imbecility, and simple incompetence is Tim Burton, who was once something resembling a great film director. The truth is that Burton has been on a downward slope for much of the last decade, but this film is not merely a new low; it is a depressingly succinct declaration that his pseudo-goth stylings and lovingly bleak visuals, which once harbored the charm and mystery of a perpetual Halloween, have now become nothing more than another product to be spewed out whenever Disney shows up with another $100 million budget. It is possible—we may hope—that Burton is building up his box office credibility in order to attempt some future project of better and more dangerous quality; but for now, ladies and gentlemen, the genius has, officially, declared himself a hack.

Originally published on March 31, 2010

The Depredations of Roger Ebert

Armond White of the *New York Press*, detractors have noted, seems to think he is the only real film critic in America. They may well be right, but probably so is he, and the *Press'* house contrarian deserves thanks from all self-respecting cinephiles for doing the one thing most (perhaps all) other American film critics either refuse to do or are incapable of doing. Whether one disagrees with White or not, and almost everybody does at one point or another, there is no question that, whatever he writes, he is always *thinking* about cinema. What it is. What is can do. What it means. This is not much in the tradition of American film criticism, which has mostly been the domain of frustrated literary or theater critics, and sometimes simply the cub reporter nobody knows what to do with. It is far more in line with the extraordinary legacy of French film criticism, especially the avatars of the *nouvelle vague* like Francois Truffaut and Jean-Luc Godard, who later became groundbreaking filmmakers in their own right.

The great insight of the French film critics was that all cinema says something about cinema, even the usually dismissed movies like Hitchcock's thrillers and Hollywood B-movies. But they did not hold simply that a B-movie could be great while an A-movie could be bad, but that all movies have something to say about cinema, and sometimes the B-movie can say something far more important and profound than an A-movie. White, it seems to me, writes according to this dictum, while most of his colleagues, if they ever encountered it, would probably have no idea what it means.

Foremost among these is unquestionably *Chicago Sun-Times* columnist, longtime television star, and all around face, voice, and personification of American film criticism, Roger Ebert. Ebert is unquestionably the most famous and probably the most successful movie reviewer in American history. Recently stricken with cancer and horribly deformed by a botched operation, and embraced, as a result, by America's high priestess of the banal, Oprah Winfrey, Ebert and his legacy are now on the verge of being all but canonized.

It has been left to Armond White, unsurprisingly, to tell the truth about that legacy. "I do think it is fair to say," /Film.com quotes him as saying, "that Roger Ebert destroyed film criticism."

> Because of the wide and far reach of television, he became an example of what a film critic does for too many people. And what he did simply was not criticism. It was simply blather. And it was a kind of purposefully dishonest enthusiasm for product, not real criticism at all. … I think he does *not* have the training. … Ebert just simply happened to have the job. And he's had the job for a long time. He does not have the foundation. He simply got the job. … Often he wasn't practicing criticism at all. Often he would point out gaffes or mistakes in continuity. That's not criticism. That's really a pea-brained kind of fan gibberish.

White is, as usual, both undiplomatic and entirely correct. Indeed, his final point is eminently borne out by Ebert's scathing review of the silly but quite enjoyable *Transformers: Revenge of the Fallen*, a film which the critical establishment, for unknown reasons, decided was a threat to human civilization. "Hello!" Ebert informs us in his standard eighth-grade prose, "you can't outrun an explosion," as if this mattered at all in an action movie. Considering that Ebert claims (with depressing predictability) that *Citizen Kane* is his favorite movie, one could just as easily point out that no one is actually in the room to hear Kane's last words that set the whole film in motion. If someone says "Rosebud" in an empty room, does it still make a sound? *Revenge of the Fallen* is, of course, nothing like the equal of *Citizen Kane*, but the point is worth making, if only for the sake of illustrating the pedantic irrelevancy of Ebert's observation.

Indeed, Ebert's own writings on *Citizen Kane* provide some valuable insight into just how pedantic and irrelevant Ebert's observations can be. Orson Welles, as many know, did everything in his power to downplay the significance of the Rosebud twist at the end of his film, and Ebert may well be deferring to this when he notes that "it explains nothing." A few sentences before, however, he expended a large number of words telling us everything it does explain: "Rosebud is the emblem of the security, hope and innocence of childhood, which a man can spend his life seeking to regain. It is the green light at the end of Gatsby's pier; the leopard atop Kilimanjaro, seeking nobody knows what; the bone tossed into the air in *2001*. It is that yearning after transience that adults learn to suppress." None of this awful pseudo-poetry amounts to much, and Ebert's final missive that "it is remarkably satisfactory as a demonstration that nothing can be explained" is nearly incomprehensible, on a par with another of his insights, "A man always seems the same size to himself, because he does not stand where we stand to look at him."

Ebert is, of course, partially correct in the most banal sense, in that Rosebud, as a simple plot point, is a symbol of lost innocence. But even the most challenged of viewers can realize this within a few seconds of the film's final shot, and Ebert's gibbering accomplishes little more than restating this at great length. And his one attempt at a deeper insight is quite simply wrong. The final images of *Kane* are clearly not a "yearning after transience," but a *lamentation on* transience. There is never the slightest indication anywhere in *Kane* that transience is something to be desired, and the sense of a lost, lamented world is something that runs throughout all of Welles's work, especially *Kane*'s immediate successor, the magnificent and mutilated *The Magnificent Ambersons*.

It is merely sad that Ebert cannot read his favorite film with any degree of accuracy. More problematic, however, is that the banality of his remarks robs his readers of any new insight into or appreciation for one of the most important and influential films ever made. Indeed, Ebert's entire take on the film can essentially be summarized as follows: "Orson Welles made this movie when he was really young. It has very good photography. It's all about trying to find out what Rosebud means. But in the end it doesn't mean anything. Which is kind of a good thing." This is a caricature, of course, but it is not much exaggerated, and it applies quite well to most of Ebert's other writings on films both great and small.

To stay with Welles for a moment, Ebert provides a good example when he writes about the director's last masterpiece, *Chimes at Midnight* (1965), a variation on Shakespeare's Falstaff plays. "The scene of the battle of Shrewsbury is justly famous," he writes. "It lasts fully 10 minutes, chaotic action at a brutal pitch, horses and men confused in smoke and fog, steel crashing against steel, cries of pain, desperate struggles, confused limbs caked in mud and blood, men falling exhausted or dead." This is, again, accurate so far as it goes. It explains next to nothing, however, about what may be the greatest and certainly one of the most influential battle scenes ever filmed.

Welles shoots the battle mostly at eye level, with what often appear to be handheld cameras. Though set and costumed in the Middle Ages, most of it looks like newsreel footage, and while it is edited to appear to be chaos, it quickly becomes clear that it has been very carefully constructed in order to evoke a kaleidoscopic, subjective experience of battle. Watching it, one sees immediately what inspired the D-Day sequence in *Saving Private Ryan*, the opening fight in *Gangs of New York*, and even some of Peckinpah's most famous set pieces.

What it provides us, moreover, is a vision of the two faces of the origins of cinema. On the one side, a battle montage worthy of Eisenstein and Griffith, and on the other, in Welles's intercuts of the plump Falstaff pratfalling his way out of danger, the physical comedy of Keaton and Chaplin. Welles's genius in this scene, in other words, is to show us just how powerful cinema, at its proper extremes, can be, and always has been. In Ebert's hands, however, it is merely a catalogue of badly described moments, given no meaning or context, and marked by such hideous deformations of grammar as "There was not something Falstaffian about Welles, there was everything."

So long as we are on the subject of battle scenes, Ebert's take on two films by the Japanese master Akira Kurosawa provides equally damning insights into the poverty of Ebert's work. Describing the central battle scene of Kurosawa's *Ran* (1985), an adaptation of *King Lear* set in medieval Japan, Ebert informs us that Kurosawa "uses several static cameras to film the action, cutting between them; because his cameras don't dart and whirl, we are not encouraged to think of ourselves as participants but as gods, observing, taking the long view here and then a closeup look." This is not wrong, *per se*, but it ignores, quite stupefyingly, the most important distancing element in the sequence, which is that it contains no live sound for half of its

49

running time. Instead, the silent images of carnage unroll with nothing behind them but an extraordinary rumbling dirge written by modernist composer Toru Takemitsu. The live sound then returns with the report of a gunshot, and the viewer is suddenly thrown headlong into the chaotic noise of war. The sequence, in effect, provides us with an object lesson in how cinema can manipulate our perceptions, keeping us at arm's length and then suddenly pulling us in, forcing us simultaneously to reckon with our reactions to the violent images Kurosawa is presenting, and to question our distance from them, a distance that is inherent in cinema itself.

Equally egregious is Ebert's inscrutable indifference to the final sequence in Kurosawa's *Kagemusha* (1980), perhaps the director's greatest accomplishment. The film tells the true story of a thief who is used by a samurai clan to impersonate their dead warlord, the charismatic Lord Shingen. "At the end," Ebert writes, "the son of the real Lord Shingen orders his troops into a suicidal charge, and their deaths are not only unnecessary but meaningless, because they are not on behalf of the sacred person of the warlord."

This is essentially all he writes about what is quite simply one of the greatest moments in cinema. The clan faces off against its enemies, who are dug in across the plain and armed with muskets. One by one, Lord Shingen's son orders his army's divisions, each named after one of the elements from Sun Tzu's *Art of War*, into battle. They charge into the field. Gunfire erupts. But Kurosawa denies us a shot of the battle itself. After the last division is exhausted, a terrifying kettle drum rumbles on to the soundtrack. And then we see it: A sea of corpses. Wounded men and horses trying to raise themselves, stumbling, and falling in slow motion. An apocalyptic vision of horror and death. Kurosawa sustains the scene for several minutes, an eternity of screen time, until it is almost unbearable to watch. He ends, finally, on the thief, who has witnessed everything and now stumbles, white-faced, toward the fallen standard of the clan. He has finally become Lord Shingen, but he is Shingen's ghost, there to witness the decimation of his army and his dreams of a united Japan. Through the simplest cinematic tools—nothing more than editing, picking and choosing what to show and when— Kurosawa denies us the vicarious excitement that usually accompanies cinematic battle scenes and instead forces us to confront the full horror of man's ability to destroy himself. It is a transcendent scene, perhaps the greatest Kurosawa ever shot, and Ebert has little more to say about it than a banal, moralistic aside that is not much more insightful than telling us that you cannot outrun an explosion.

To be fair, it should be noted that Ebert's career has not been entirely without merit. He championed Scorsese before it was fashionable, and has taken the occasional unpopular stand, most notably on behalf of Sam Peckinpah's demented classic *Bring Me the Head of Alfredo Garcia* (1974) which occasioned one of Ebert's few genuinely insightful remarks. "Courage usually feels good in the movies," he writes, and he is right, "but it comes in many moods, and here it feels bad but necessary, giving us a hero who is heartbreakingly human—a little man determined to accomplish his mission in memory of a woman he loved, and in truth to his own defiant code." Somewhat maudlin, perhaps, but an admirable sentiment nonetheless, and worth being reminded of.

Such moments are few and far between in Ebert's work, however, and perusing it, one is struck throughout by what can only be described as a persistent inability—or perhaps refusal—to actually *think* about what he is watching, and to provide his readers with something more than a mere reiteration of events and a handful of apparently arbitrary judgments. Ebert's theory of cinema in effect amounts to little more than "I liked this, I didn't like that." Or, perhaps, "This happened, and I liked it. Then this happened, and I didn't like it."

This is cataloguing, not criticism, and while it may lend itself to the fast-food style of movie reviewing that assigns stars and a thumbs up or down, it abdicates entirely the role and responsibility of the critic, which is to discern what the object of his criticism is, what it says about itself and its medium, and what it says, also, about we who are witnessing it and the society that created it. Ebert has made pale and stumbling attempts at one or two of these things, and they merely serve to throw his limitations into ever more devastating relief. When it comes to America and it's often fraught relationship with what may be its greatest art form, Roger Ebert is heard everywhere; but, ironically and unfortunately, he has proved to have remarkably little to say.

Tintin, Herge, and the Shadow of Innocence

The news that Steven Spielberg and Peter Jackson will soon be producing a series of films based on the Belgian comics character Tintin has given more than a few of us — and in the Anglophone world, we are indeed few — some pause. We are those who, from our childhoods, have enjoyed considering ourselves the members of a rarified group lucky enough to enjoy the exploits of this enigmatic piece of European pop culture. Tintin has never taken off in America, and probably never will, despite the best efforts of Mr. Spielberg, who is, if he is nothing else, a master popularizer.

The truth is that Tintin has always been the Gallic hero par excellence. There is nothing remotely American about him. And what those of us who love the character and revere his creator — the melancholic and childlike Herge — have always responded to has been precisely that. For us, Tintin was our earliest window into another world. A world far older, more compromised, more frightening, and more pessimistic than the wide-open dreamscape of American pop culture. A world infused with the ever-presence of the political and that particularly European sense of crisis. Tintin's world is a fantastic landscape that is always in danger of collapse before real-world forces and real-world violence. There could be nothing that is further from the phantasmagoria of the American superhero comics, with their ubermenschen laying waste to the forces of evil, always rendered, even in the supposedly "grim and gritty" genre, as incredulous grosteques, their evil made manifest by their physical deformity and the derangement of their actions.

This was Herge's genius. His world of adventure is an inversion of the original. The traditional children's tale brings the adult world into that of the child, so that it is forced to play by a child's rules: the manic bursts of energy, the corrosive violence of an unfettered and unapologetic Id, authority and evil as mere caricatures of themselves. Herge brought the child's world into that of the adult.

In the person of Tintin, he creates a character who is neither child nor adult, but an interloper, an androgynous, sexless blank, a neutral center around which the mad, frightening spectacle of the adult world revolves.

Herge's deeply troubled and ambivalent Catholicism was Tintin's true creator. He is utterly free of original sin. He has no neuroses, no doubts, no ideology per se, indeed, no thoughts of his own whatsoever. Much like the child, he is an innocent voyager through a mysterious world. No doubt, Tintin was one-half Herge. The world he created around his character was the other.

This is the opposite of the American superhero, who dominates his surroundings and everyone in it. Tintin dominates nothing. Such a character is almost unknown in the Anglophone world, but in Continental terms he is eminently understandable. He is the creature of the spectacle, the alien blank on to which the audience can project itself; the figure toward whom empathy is impossible, thus emphasizing his surroundings and forcing us to contemplate their full implications.

Nowhere does this appear more profoundly than in Bilal's brilliant pastiche of Tintin escaping unknown enemies through a cyberpunk sewer, Snowy perched precariously on his shoulder, his hand clutching an impossibly massive blaster gun. The most striking aspect of this image is how strangely appropriate it seems. Tintin, in his nothingness, has only ever been a guide through exotic surroundings. One could insert him into any frame of *Blade Runner* without incongruence. Probably the only place he would seem out of place is a strip club.

This is likely how Herge wanted it. Tintin may be the only modern work of art which is completely impervious to Freud. There is excitement, and to a certain extent desire, but there is not a trace of the erotic. Herge himself insisted that the primary value of his books was friendship, which seems entirely appropriate. Friendship is the only form of human solidarity outside the family which is characterized by both passionate love and complete asexuality. It is, for the Catholic, even a bad one, the purest form of human love, untainted by desire, carnality, and sin. It is the closest the flesh can come to the world of the spirit. Except, of course, for the world of the child's imagination, which is Tintin's only true home.

This imagination, however, was a purity which Herge populated with corruptions—with Japanese spies, scheming Bordurians, pathetically deranged South American dictators, and any and all manner of malfeasants, both the malicious and the inadvertently irritating. This entertaining but vaguely sadistic need to populate the innocent mind with the horrors of the adult world reveals the schism at the heart of Herge's work and at the heart of Herge. There is always the brutal world. A world of drug-dealers and slave traders, of murders which occur regularly, if always safely out of sight, the permanent threat of some looming war or grotesque perversion of natural justice. And, of course, there are Mitsuhirato, Rastapopoulos, Allan, Carriedias—a cast of sadists and criminals who are the match of the most fervid imagination.

It is impossible not to conclude from this that, whatever may have remained in him of his youthful Catholicism, by middle age Herge had long since lost his faith. Nowhere is this more pronounced than in his famous dispute with Casterman over Wolff's final sacrifice in *Explorers on the Moon*. "Perhaps by some miracle," Herge was made to make Wolff say, "I shall escape too." "The guy is doomed," was Herge's verdict on this unwilling revision, "out there in that emptiness…"

This emptiness was the landscape of Herge's own despair. In the 1950s he sank into a melancholy typified by terrifying, featureless dreams of pure whiteness. As if the blankness of his most famous character had invaded his inner self. A psychiatrist told him that he had to exorcise a "purity demon." Instead, he sent his hero straight into that absolute white. Perhaps he never quite brought him back. The most extraordinary scene Herge ever drew is contained in *Tintin in Tibet*, the most idiosyncratic and disturbing of all the books. Trapped in a Himalayan snowstorm, unable to find his way back to camp, Tintin moves relentlessly onward to keep from freezing. The white of the snow and the white of the landscape merge, so there are no landmarks, no features by which to navigate. He could be walking in circles or off the edge of the world. He is lost in the purest sense. And then, a dark shape, a mere shadow emerges out of the white. He calls to it in desperation, but it does not answer. This moment is pure dream. A perfect synthesis of symbol, allegory, realism, and suffering. Tintin, the untroubled, uncomplicated, unsuffering hero, is forced to confront his own purity, and out of the purity emerges the shadow self. Like Reinhold Messner's famous phantom companions, who would accompany him in the last hours of his oxygenless climbs, this is the briefest glimpse of the doppelganger, the purity demon who emerges—dark, ominous, and mute—out of the white. The *ligne clair* fails, at last, in that moment in the snow. Like Tintin, we cannot see.

If this sublime and unique moment teaches us anything, it is that Herge was unquestionably an artist. Toiling, perhaps, in the trenches of lowbrow pop culture, but an artist nonetheless. Art, after all, is simply dreams brought into focus. The compulsive filling in of details in order to delineate what are initially only vague and disturbing impressions.

Of course, both Spielberg and Jackson have shown the occasional moment of inadvertent artistry. They may succeed in making more of Tintin than we imagine, or Tintin may succeed in making more of them. But it seems doubtful that they will be able to translate what was, after all, one man's struggle against the demons of his own innocence, into something of commensurate beauty. Herge, I think, will remain unsullied, in that moment of snow-blindness, by seeing.

Originally published on February 6, 2009

www.ingramcontent.com/pod-product-compliance
Lightning Source LLC
Chambersburg PA
CBHW051223170526
45166CB00005B/2024